GO FACTS OCEANS
People and the Sea

A & C BLACK • LONDON

People and the Sea

© Blake Publishing Pty Ltd 2002
Additional Material © A & C Black Publishers Ltd 2003

First published 2002 in Australia by Blake Education Pty Ltd

This edition published 2003 in the United Kingdom by
A&C Black Publishers Ltd, 37 Soho Square, London W1D 3QZ
www.acblack.com

ISBN 0-7136-6613-7

A CIP record for this book is available from the British Library.

Written by Sharon Dalgleish and Garda Turner
Science Consultant: Dr Will Edwards, James Cook University
Design and layout by The Modern Art Production Group
Photos by Photodisc, Stockbyte, John Foxx, Corbis, Imagin,
Artville Digital Vision and Corel

UK Series Consultant: Julie Garnett

Printed in Hong Kong by Wing King Tong Co Ltd

A & C Black uses paper produced with elemental chlorine-free pulp,
harvested from managed sustainable forests.

Explorers

From early times people have set sail on the oceans to explore the unknown. Some explorers looked for new lands to settle. Others looked for adventure, treasure or fame.

More than 3 000 years ago people explored the Pacific Ocean. In small canoes, people used the stars to find their way. By the early 1200s the magnetic compass had been invented. Sailors could then navigate more easily. Even so, the journeys were still filled with danger.

Long before science helped us understand the oceans, people thought the Earth was flat. Sailors believed that if they sailed far enough, they would fall off the edge of the world. Of course they never did, but storms, pirates and hidden reefs meant that some ships did sink to the bottom of the sea. Today, adventurers go in search of the sunken treasure!

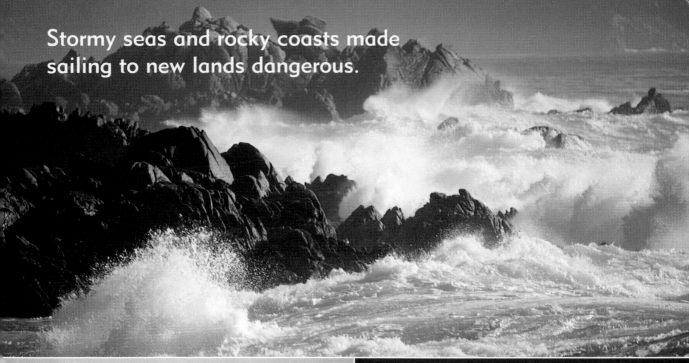

Stormy seas and rocky coasts made sailing to new lands dangerous.

Early boats were very simple.

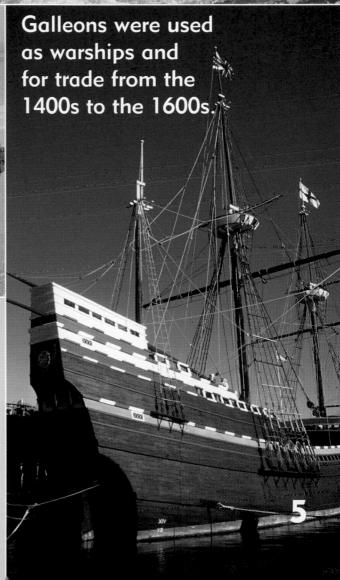

Galleons were used as warships and for trade from the 1400s to the 1600s.

GO FACTS

DID YOU KNOW?

Ferdinand Magellan's ships were the first to sail around the world. Magellan set sail from Spain in 1519 with five ships. In 1522 only one of his ships made it home.

Water Pressure

The water pressure in the deep sea is extremely high. Deep-sea water pressure would crush a person.

Try this experiment to see how **water pressure** increases in deeper water.

You will need:
- deep bucket
- straw or plastic tube
- water and food colouring
- balloon
- elastic band

What to do:

1. Fill the bucket with water.

2. Attach the straw or plastic tube to the balloon with an elastic band. Fill the balloon with coloured water.

3. Slowly lower the balloon into the bucket.

4. Watch the level of the coloured water as you push the balloon deeper.

Now try this:
Wrap your hand in a plastic bag and place your hand under the water. You will feel the pressure increase as you push your hand deeper into the water.

Just below the surface, the water pressure is low.

Deeper down, the water pressure pushes the water from the balloon into the tube.

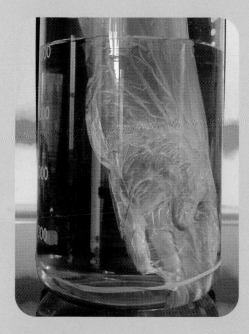

The water pressure presses the plastic around your hand.

GO FACTS

DID YOU KNOW?

Deep-sea divers need to wear special suits to protect themselves from the crushing water pressure.

Food from the Sea

People have always caught fish and other sea creatures using baskets, hooks and nets. Today, large fishing boats can catch, clean and freeze fish while still at sea.

Modern fishing boats take huge amounts of seafood from the sea. Popular ocean fish that people eat include tuna, herring, sardines, cod and snapper. Every year about 75 million tonnes of fish are caught worldwide.

fishmonger

Seaweed is also **harvested**. People eat it raw or cooked and sometimes use it to thicken foods such as ice-cream and yoghurt. Seaweed can also be used to make toothpaste and sausages!

In some hot countries, people trap sea water in shallow ponds. The sun and wind dry up the water, leaving behind the salt. The salt is collected and used to season and preserve food.

Large fishing boats use a tracking system called sonar, to find large schools of fish.

Many people use small boats to go fishing.

This man is harvesting seaweed.

Energy from the Sea

Almost a quarter of the oil and natural gas we use comes from beneath the sea. Oil and gas are fossil fuels that people use to make heat and power.

Fossil fuels are the remains of long-dead plants and animals that were preserved in a rock-like form. Millions of years ago, plants and tiny sea creatures died and sank to the bottom of the ocean. The plants and animals were slowly pressed together. Then heat and pressure changed them into natural gas or oil.

Geologists drill holes in the ocean floor, looking for oil and gas. When a large amount of oil or gas is found, a platform is built in the open sea. Narrow holes are drilled into the seabed. The oil or gas is then pumped to the surface. Oil is loaded into big ships called tankers. Natural gas is sent to the shore by pipeline.

There are large oil platforms in the ocean.

Large pipes carry gas across the land for use or for storage.

These men are drilling for oil on an oil rig.

GO FACTS

DID YOU KNOW?

Oil and gas are running out so the world needs new sources of energy, such as sun and wind.

Working at Sea

If you're looking for an easy time, you may not want to work at sea. Some people think the ocean is a great place to find a career — full of excitement and discovery.

An oil platform is like a small city at sea. Hundreds of people live on the platform surrounded by the drilling equipment, pumps and power plant. The platform also has living areas with places to sleep, eat and play.

A **research** ship is a floating laboratory. A large research ship needs a crew of up to twenty people. Thirty different scientists may also live and work on board.

scientist

Scientists study what lives in the water and on the sea floor. They also study how water moves in the oceans and how the oceans affect the **atmosphere**.

You could join the navy to have a life working at sea. You could also become a boatbuilder, engineer, lighthouse keeper, fisher, diver or even a ship's cook.

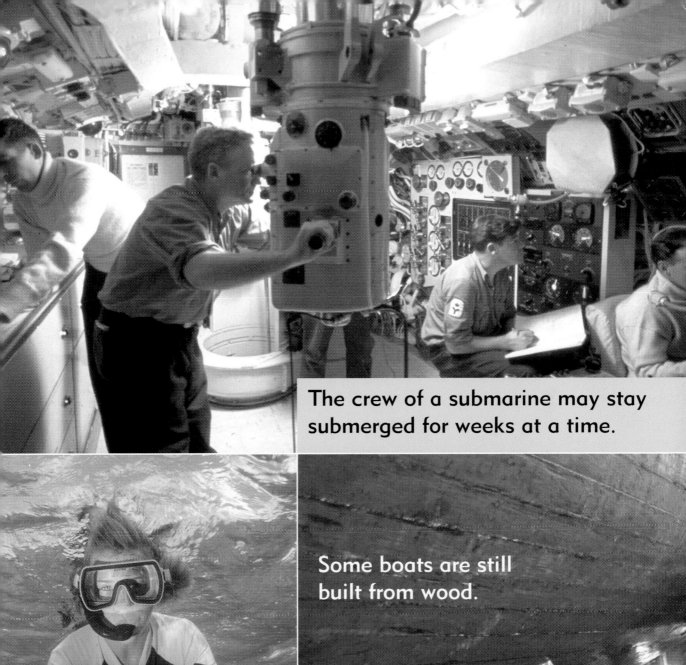

The crew of a submarine may stay submerged for weeks at a time.

Divers explore ocean life.

Some boats are still built from wood.

Ocean Highways

Ships used to be small and made of wood. Today they are large, powerful and made of steel. World trade depends on ships to carry goods around the world.

Ocean and sea routes are like water motorways. Ships follow special **shipping lanes** around the world. Each day, tankers carry oil from the Middle East to the rest of the world. Bulk carriers transport iron ore, coal, food and manufactured goods from one country to another. Cruise ships carry passengers on holiday.

With all this traffic, the shipping lanes can get very busy. So busy, there is a danger of ships colliding with each other! To solve the problem, ships have **radar** and **sonar** equipment. They also use radio waves sent via **satellite** to guide them. When the ships get close to land, lighthouses and marker **buoys** help them get to port safely.

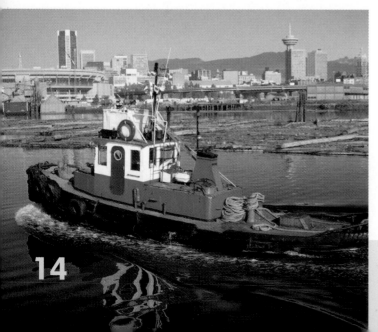

14

tugboat

Tugboats guide large ships into port.

Icebreakers are special boats that can travel through ice fields.

15

The Wild Sea

Some of the wildest storms on Earth begin at sea. When these storms hit land, they can cause terrible destruction.

Cyclones form over very warm seas. Water vapour rises and creates clouds. As the rising clouds get bigger, more warm air comes in from the bottom. Then the storm clouds start to spin.

These huge, spinning wind storms bring heavy rain and are very destructive. For ships at sea, cyclones are a great danger. When a cyclone hits land, it can cause terrible damage over a large area.

Tsunamis are giant waves caused by earthquakes in the seabed. When a tsunami gets close to land, the giant wave begins to crest and break. As the water gets shallower, the waves bump against the seabed and get higher and higher. Finally, the sea is sucked from the shore before the waves come rushing back as a giant wall of water.

Spinning cyclones can be seen from space.

Houses can be completely destroyed by cyclones.

GO FACTS

DID YOU KNOW?

A tsunami can travel across deep oceans as fast as a jet plane! The waves can be up to 65 metres high when they hit land.

Oceans in Trouble

Ocean pollution and overfishing are major problems. People need to work together to protect the oceans of the world.

The world's rivers and oceans are all connected. If chemical pollution from factories is dumped into rivers, it flows into the ocean. Whatever people put down a drain also ends up in the ocean. Even chemical sprays used on farms can seep through the ground and end up in the ocean. We cannot always see the pollution, but it can be deadly.

In 1989 a huge tanker, Exxon Valdez, struck a reef. It spilled 50 million litres of oil into the ocean. Oil spills like this are disastrous. The water is poisoned and sea creatures die. Animals also die when their feathers or fur get coated in oil.

Some laws have been passed to help protect the oceans. By working together, people can succeed in protecting the ocean and its wonderful wildlife.

Ships pollute the oceans by discharging waste.

GO FACTS

DID YOU KNOW?

The Exxon Valdez oil spill covered more that 2 500 km of Alaskan shoreline. It killed at least 580 000 seabirds, and 5 500 sea and river otters.

This sea otter is covered in oil after an oil spill.

Enjoying the Sea

People enjoy activities such as swimming, surfing, scuba diving and boating. Simple rules help keep everyone safe.

At the beach, swimmers should follow the lifeguards' instructions. Surfers must stay away from swimming areas. If the waves are too rough or too big, don't swim.

Scuba divers must make sure their equipment is working properly before going on each dive. They also learn hand signals so they can communicate with other divers under water. No-one should dive alone.

There are special rules for people who like boating.

1. Make sure the boat is in good condition.

2. Plan your trip. Know where you are going and how long you will be. Tell someone else of your plans.

3. Check the weather forecast. Make sure it is safe boating weather.

4. Wear a life jacket.

5. Carry a first aid kit, torch, distress flares and a towrope. A radio that lets you talk to someone on shore is a good idea.

Surfers must stay clear of swimmers.

People in boats have to watch swimmers and people snorkelling.

Sunscreen and shade protect your skin from sunburn.

21

Using the Sea

Food

Energy

Recreation

Transportation

Glossary

atmosphere	the mixture of gases that surrounds Earth
buoy	an anchored marker that floats
fossil fuel	remains of plants and animals that have turned into oil and coal
geologist	someone who studies rocks
harvested	gathered grains or other live foods
radar	a positioning device that sends out radio waves and measures the time taken for the echo to return
satellite	an object that orbits Earth and sends and receives information
scuba	**s**elf **c**ontained **u**nderwater **b**reathing **a**pparatus
shipping lanes	regular routes that ships follow
sonar	equipment that uses sound waves to determine depth or position
tsunami	a large wave caused by an undersea earthquake
water pressure	pressure caused by the weight of water above

Index